My dear Jill,

I just Loved _____

and I think You will also.

Its a Book you Can read over and over!

I hope you Enjoy It!

My Love
Always, - your Mom -
& OF COURSE
" SANDLER "

A home is just a Shelter
without a dog!

Good Dog. Stay.

ANNA QUINDLEN

RANDOM HOUSE

NEW YORK

Published in the United States by Random House,
an imprint of The Random House Publishing Group,
a division of Random House, Inc., New York.

RANDOM HOUSE and colophon are
registered trademarks of Random House, Inc.

LIBRARY OF CONGRESS
CATALOGING-IN-PUBLICATION DATA

Quindlen, Anna.

Good Dog. Stay / Anna Quindlen.

p. cm.

ISBN 978-1-4000-6713-8

1. Quindlen, Anna. 2. Authors—20th century—
Biography.
3. Pet owner—United States—Biography.
4. Human-animal relationships.
5. Labrador Retriever. I. Title.

PS3567.U336Z46 2007

818'.5403—dc22   2007031820

Printed in the United States of America on acid-free paper

www.atrandom.com

2 4 6 8 9 7 5 3 1

FIRST EDITION

Book design by Barbara M. Bachman

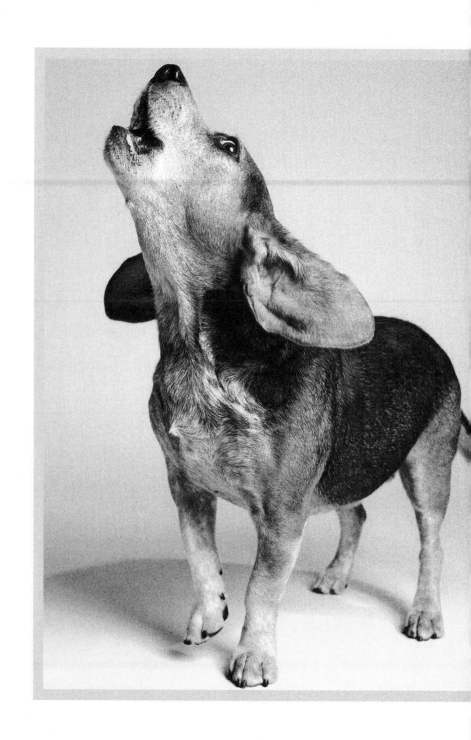

*F*or several years I was that most pathetic of creatures, a human who walks into the veterinarian's office without an animal. "Beau?" the woman behind the desk would call, and I would rise. Dr. Brown would usher me back into an examining room kitted out with a bottle of preserved heartworms and a model of the canine knee and send me off with a prescription refill and the promise of a house call when necessary. The house call would be for the purpose of euthanasia, but neither of us ever said the word.

The object of our discussion, a black Labrador retriever with the ridiculous AKC name Bristol's Beauregard Buchanan, was at home sleeping on an oriental rug in the foyer. The rug smelled. So did Beau. At this late date there was not much reason for him to appear at the vet in person. His sight and his hearing were mostly gone. But he had retained the uncanny ability to know when a certain phony lilt to my voice as I snapped on the leash meant we were headed to that place where his prostate was once examined. After that memorable visit, when he emerged from the back of the veterinary office with the fur on his spine raised as though he was a Rhodesian ridgeback, he had made me a figure of fun on crowded New York City streets. "You're really pulling that dog," a man once said, stating the obvious near a bus stop on Broadway. It was true; Beau's white-coat syndrome took the form of systemic paralysis, so that he turned himself into a solid seventy-five-pound block at the end of the leash, like one of those wooden pull toys for children, but bigger and more obdurate. When we finally made it to the waiting room, he would begin to shake and shiver and shed his coat, so that the other patients and their people were enveloped in a haze of fine black fur not unlike a cloud of gnats.

I did not miss those forays, although I mourned the increasing infirmity that made them impossi-

ble. As Beau grew old there was no way, other than the dog taxi that advertised on the vet's bulletin board alongside the cards for homeless kittens and lost mongrels, to travel those few blocks. He moved as though his back legs were prosthetics to which he had yet to become accustomed. The very last time he sensed we might be heading to the dog doctor, he lay down on the front stoop and refused to budge. He wasn't going to make that mistake again. Neither was I. I've put in my time around people whose bodies were failing, who were clearly marooned in some limbo between illness and death. I hated the way the medical profession felt obliged to continue to poke, to test, to treat, even when cure or comfort was not in the cards. With people, it's assumed you'll do everything; with animals you have the luxury of doing the right thing. A Supreme Court justice once said that one of the most important rights is the right to be left alone. After nearly fifteen years of loyal companionship, Beau had earned that right.

It's a shame that obituaries and eulogies come only after people are gone and unable to appreciate

the class of dogs who do those kinds of jobs are still called working dogs, but most of them don't work anymore in those particular ways, nor do many hunting dogs hunt. (The classification of certain animals as toy dogs, however, remains accurate.) The job so many dogs really perform is to allow us to project our feelings upon them, to assume they are excited or downhearted or lonely when we are. "He's so much happier when he's out in the country," my husband always liked to say about Beau. And maybe he was right. But I suspect it is he who is happier in the country, and he liked the idea that he and Beau were of one mind.

People do this with their children, too, trying to use them as a mirror or a foil, which is how you come to have otherwise sane men screaming instructions on Little League fields or women allowing preadolescent girls to wear just a little lip gloss, just a little blush. Most parents come to their senses sooner rather than later, so that their sons and daughters are not forced into a declaration of independence and individuality by leaving home or

marrying young. But any woman who has ever lain in a birthing room and watched as, in violation of all laws of physics, an entire human being emerged from her body, can be forgiven if she has a difficult time seeing the resulting person as utterly and irreversibly separate.

For a long time I thought of myself, rather smugly, as quite good at this separation stuff. Then one evening I was providing what, it developed, was some heavy-handed help on a high school essay. In an even tone of voice, our daughter said, "Mom, I am not you." Along with "Will you marry me?" and "You're pregnant," those words are a flag flying in my subconscious from here to eternity.

Dogs, however, do not talk, or talk back, which is part of their charm in a hyperverbal age, and so they lend themselves effortlessly and endlessly to this sort of projection. So does their essential open-faced affect. It would never occur to me to assume that the cat and I have two hearts that beat as one; with his narrowed amber eyes and scarred upper lip, his prevailing mode is either contempt or indif-

ference. When he curls around my ankles, it suggests hunger, not affection. I like this about cats; they're the Clint Eastwoods of companion animals. A dog who sits by your side craves company; a cat is doing you a favor. This is why when you say "Sit!" a cat rises and stalks out of the room. Most dogs will fall back onto their haunches, vibrating slightly, their liquid eyes locked on yours.

Human beings wind up having the relationship with dogs that they fool themselves they will have with other people. When we are very young, it is the perfect communion we honestly believe we will have with a lover; when we are older, it is the symbiosis we manage to fool ourselves we will always have with our children. Love unconditional, attention unwavering, companionship without question or criticism. I once saw a pillow that said I WOULD LIKE TO BE THE MAN MY DOG THINKS I AM. That about covers it.

So the traits we ascribe to our dogs, the stories we tell ourselves about them are, at some level, our own stories. When Beau tottered down our block, passersby saw a very old Lab with a white muzzle and a tail that seemed vaguely broken, as though all those years of wagging had worn it out. But I saw a dog whose entire life, puppyhood to adolescence to middle and old age, was inextricably entwined with those of two little boys with high, piping voices and their younger sister, who spent her formative years trailing her brothers around. I remember the three of them squatting next to a roly-poly puppy and allowing him to gnaw on their fingers. "He has really sharp teeth," the eldest said. "You're right, Quin," said the second. "His teeth are really sharp!" "Really sharp," their sister repeated.

Those boys are men, the girl a woman, their parents middle-aged. That is the story of my life, and of Beau's. His children grew tall, their familiar voices dropped in tone and timbre, their soft faces sharpened to reveal the architecture of cheekbones and chin. But he always knew them. They went away to college, were gone for months at a time, spilled back through the door with a clutch of friends so enamored of their own lives that sometimes they

merely stepped over him on their way to somewhere else. And still his tail thrummed on the hardwood floor, like the fan belt on some machine.

Sometimes people tell me that their children are begging for a puppy, and that they won't be fooled into going along because they know, they *know* that the kids say they will train the dog, walk the dog, feed and brush and tend the dog, but they won't. Well, of course they won't. Any parents who believe that they themselves will not wind up walking the dog most, if not all, of the time—especially in a downpour or a sleet storm—are parents who will also believe that there is no homework over the winter break and that the cigarettes belonged to someone else. For children, the point of having a dog is something like the point of having a mother and father. Our job is not to do but to be, not to act but to exist. We are bedrock, scenery, landscape, to be often ignored and then clung to during difficult or frightening or, occasionally, happy times. My mom, my dad, my dog, my home, immutable, to leave and then to return to at will and leave again.

Once he'd grown to adulthood, Beau was the sort of dog whom central casting might have chosen for that solid and stable role, with his big blocky head, foursquare stance, gruff bark. A Disney cartoonist could have anthropomorphized him, in robes or a white coat, as a judge or a general practitioner. But his long Labrador life started off wild and crazy. We mothers do not use the word "bad" much anymore, believing that it is too judgmental in a nonjudgmental age. Instead we use the locution "not good," as in "Christopher, it is so not good for you to put yogurt in Maria's hair. Quin, it is so not good that you told him to do that." In his formative years, Beau was so not good that nothing and no one was safe. Friends who came to visit in the country had to be repeatedly cautioned not to leave shoes or socks at ground level when they wanted to go swimming; he ate them both. My most enduring memory of his youth is of him galloping around the yard, purloined needlepoint yarn streaming from his mouth. As an adolescent dog he once happily grabbed our daughter by her ponytail and tried to

run off with her. He looked completely flummoxed when we screamed at him and, I am sad to say now, thrashed him with a rolled newspaper.

My husband likes to say that there are no bad dogs, only bad masters, although usually when he says this he is not talking about dogs at all. Occasionally we had to wonder if we were bad masters. Beau ran away and we had to leave the country for the city without him one Sunday evening while the children sobbed in the backseat. "Is Beau dead?" asked the eldest as the wailing music of the other two, like one of those discordant modern compositions, grew louder. We put an ad in the local paper and it turned out that Beau was not dead but living happily with a golden retriever about two miles away. My father drove his pickup there with Beau's crate in the back and dragged him home. Even in the less hospitable city, if the door to the house was left open for even a moment he would slip out and gallop, unfettered, down the street. I would run for blocks, with passersby to guide me: Oh, the black dog? He went that way. One wag suggested I write a children's book entitled "Follow That Dog!" I did not find it funny.

Labradors are notorious late bloomers, dogs who continue to think they are puppies long past the statutory age and weight at which this seems reasonable. The most frequent advice we received was that Beau would stay much closer to home after he was fixed, a strange term of art, since it suggests that a male with all his parts working is a problem in need of a remedy. Fixed he was, a simple operation accompanied by a difficult conversation. What Beau had lost had great meaning to the boys, then ten and eight; they visibly tensed as they sat side by side on the sofa. Beau himself banged around the house in

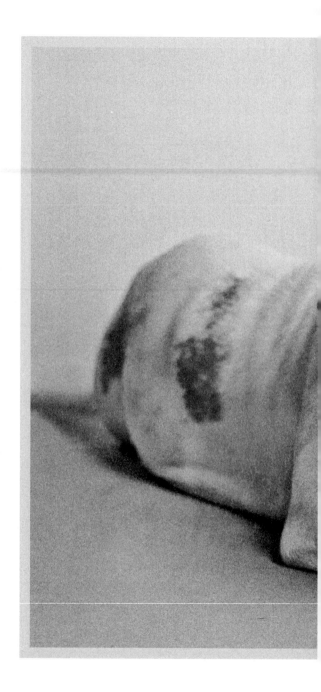

one of those plastic postsurgical collars, getting stuck in doorways, knocking mugs off the coffee table. "Old Bucket Head," we called him.

It is true that once he had grown into his tremendous feet and his tremendous tail, he settled down considerably. His circuit narrowed, from the whole wide world to the house down the road where the owners forgot to put the lids on the garbage can, and the back swamp, where there was always some chance of running into a deer carcass. Some days he would emerge, wagging wildly, with an entire rib cage in his mouth. And he still had a predilection for certain sorts of trouble. One summer he was skunked three times, and he spent weeks studded with spines after indulging his taste for advanced decomposition by rolling on a dead porcupine.

He hated horses and could hear them long before we could; he would begin to bay ceaselessly a good three or four minutes before the clip-clop of hooves would echo through the valley. Beau was also terrified by the percussive: Gunfire and thunder undid him completely, and when displays of fire-

works could be heard on the Fourth of July, it was a cinch that he would disappear upstairs. There are few things more pitiable than the sight of a full-grown Labrador with only his tail and his back end visible from beneath the dust ruffle on the bed. And he simply would not swim, no matter how often he was lectured by his master about the responsibilities of a water dog. We concluded he was defective, missing a key Labrador gene. Then one July day when he was six years old, he suddenly entered the water and began to paddle purposefully across the pond to chase away a dozen geese whose honking had enraged him.

By then he was a good dog, and we told him so often. It was one of the terms he recognized, along with "chow," "leash," and "walk." He ran with his master every morning, posed in front of the fireplace in winter in a recumbent position like an insurance ad, stayed off the furniture, and did not jump on guests. People admired his self-control, on the street and at dinner parties, although one New

Year's Eve he was discovered with his muzzle buried to the ears in a bowl of chocolate truffles.

His greatest challenge, at least until he found himself unable to negotiate the stairs, came when he was nine years old. Mesmerized by a litter of tawny puppies, we decided to acquire a yellow Labrador whose full name, Endless Mountains Biggie Shortie, was shortened to Bea. This was a mistake, since when strangers on the street asked for their names, our two dogs wound up sounding like a vaudeville act. But the biggest error, as far as Beau was concerned, was the initial impulse. Our sense was that we were doing him a tremendous favor: In his often dull and uneventful middle age, we were giving him his own dog. His sense was that we had lost our minds.

We are not the sort of people who confuse dogs with children. We never referred to ourselves as Beau's mommy and daddy, nor did we ever call him our son. We had sons, and they never tried to lick our faces nor steal hamburger meat defrosting on the kitchen counter. The chances of either my husband or I ever putting clothes on a dog is between

zero and nil. We would not be the people for a dog who would stand for such a thing.

But Beau's reaction to the acquisition of Bea was familiar to us, not from our years as dog owners but from our years as parents. He didn't like the competition. He would insinuate himself between Bea and his master every chance he got. Put a hand on her head and he was right there, using his big skull and shoulders to shift her aside. As this puppy circled his legs, nipping at his flanks and then playfully running away, he became increasingly annoyed, until finally he held her down with one paw and growled.

She learned her lesson in subservience well; she followed him everywhere slavishly and developed a habit of occasionally stopping to lick his face while he was sleeping. The dynamic was familiar to any parent. I remember once explaining to our eldest that he would have to be patient with my divided responsibilities. "Don't forget, I'm Christopher's mommy, too, Quin," I said. "And Daddy is Christopher's daddy?" he replied, horrified. It turned out that there is an enormous difference between telling a toddler a new baby is coming and having him understand that the baby is going to have dibs on the parents he believed were his alone. Or, as Christopher once went on to say about Maria, "Why did we need another baby in this house?"

Our rationale was that Bea would keep Beau young, and I suspect that is what did happen. He ran because she did, foraged at her side, kept up when he might have lain down. When both of them were younger, she used to dance in circles and butt-check her older companion violently for her own amusement, but as he became increasingly infirm she knew not to do that anymore. And while birth order meant that we called him the Big Guy, and her the Little Girl, over time she became stronger and more formidable than he. In the fashion of the frail elderly, he seemed to shrink, and his skeleton became more prominent until eventually he was all vertebrae and pelvis beneath the flat black fur. For long periods he lay, alert, his milky eyes gazing mysteriously inward, as though he was reliving the past.

Unless we entered the room with heavy footfalls he often did not know we were there, and it became important to approach him slowly so that he would not be startled by a pat on the head. Sometimes he splayed frog-legged on the linoleum and could not rise again without a boost in the rear; some days he had to be wheelbarrowed up the stairs in a kind of three-legged-race arrangement, in which we would hold his two back legs and he would use his front ones. Beau once had a catcher's mitt of a mouth, but there came a time when a scrap thrown in his direction usually bounced unseen off his head. Yet put a pork roast in the oven, and the guy still breathed as audibly as an obscene caller. The eyes and ears may have gone, but the nose was eternal. And the tail. The tail still wagged, albeit at half-staff. When it stops, I thought more than once, then we'll know.

Beau was a gift on my fortieth birthday from my closest friend and her husband. Every ten years my own husband gives me a surprise party, although, if life were a yearbook, I would overwhelmingly be voted Least Likely to Want to Be Caught Unawares.

pregnant, busy but no longer crazed. No one was in diapers; everyone was in school. My hair had not yet begun to go gray. My life was in a kind of equipoise.

All I really needed was a dog. For the first time since I graduated from college, we were dogless. For a while we had had three at once. I began with a cocker spaniel named Dollar, whom I had chosen because she was the runt of the litter. Soon I learned that if you choose a puppy out of pity, you may well wind up with a crazy dog trying always to prove her mettle, or, as we liked to say to our friends, "She will cross the room to bite a small child." Proving that dogs are better at reading people than people are at reading dogs, she stopped that behavior when the small children belonged to us, else she might have wound up at that mythical farm in the country to which parents took unwanted dogs when I was young.

Next came a golden retriever owned by a group of twentysomethings who realized, too late, that the demands of dog ownership and a life of work, parties, restaurants, and clubs did not mesh. One of their number advertised in my office: FREE, TO GOOD HOME, words that are second only to "shoe sale" in their ability to cause me to acquire that which I do not need nor can truly afford. Jason was an enormous redhead so good and gentle that he could have been a pediatric nurse had he had opposable thumbs.

Finally there was the shaggy black mutt, the companion of a squatter who died intestate in an abandoned building around the corner. "We'll take care of the dog," said the police officers removing the body, which is another version of that farm story. Instead I carried Pudgy home. By the time my husband had returned from work the children had already bonded, and his objections were for naught. I figured that if having two dogs was chaotic, one more wouldn't make much of a difference. I conveniently forgot to remember that people only have two hands, or, as another parent once said of having a third child, it's time for a zone defense instead of man-to-man.

Dollar, Jason, Pudgy. When you saw one of us on the street, struggling with three leashes, it

seemed we were just one dog away from becoming crazy dog people. Then, one by one, they grew old and died. Soon there was a little pet cemetery on the hill by the corn crib, with homemade headstones of cracked roof slates inscribed with chalk.

Occasionally someone will tell me that they won't have pets because they're messy, and I suppose there's some truth to that, between the fur and the slobber and the occasional puddle on the floor. I have to choke down the temptation to respond that life is messy, and that its vagaries go down hardest with those who fool themselves into thinking they can keep it neat. But the truth is that we were far messier without dogs than with them. After Pudgy died, when the click of claws on the floor was merely a spectral phenomenon, I discovered that the children dropped more in the kitchen than they ate. I had never noticed how many goldfish crackers, Cheerios, and crusts tumbled off the table. That was because they were either snagged in midair or gobbled as soon as they hit the ground. Dogs make messes, it's true, but they clean them up as well.

So a month after my fortieth birthday party and less than eight weeks after Pudgy died, I found myself in the birthing suite of a kennel in New Jersey, where the breeder's favorite female had produced a dozen puppies. As I sat down amid the scrambling, wriggling, wagging, and woofing, the mother rose wearily and left the room, her midsection and her muzzle drooping. The puppies had hospital bracelets around their necks with numbers on them, numbers that reflected the order in which they had been whelped. The puppy who kept clambering into my lap and looking quizzically into my face was number eleven. When I had taken number eleven home and named him Beau, I began to get a taste of what his mother's life was like. For two weeks

he woke every morning at 4:45 A.M., letting loose with a sharp little yip. Housebreaking a puppy and toilet-training a child have this in common: The adult in charge is made to feel absurd because of the need to praise the most basic bodily functions. "You are such a good boy," I would murmur, freezing in the dew-drenched grass as the night eked out its closing hours, remembering the deep and endless darkness during nighttime infant feedings as Beau danced a puppy dance under the stars.

Life is a great mystery, that's for sure. If anyone had described all this to me when I was twenty, I would have scoffed at that domestic routine. When I was thirty those children were just a gleam in our eyes; at forty I had only the vaguest notion of who they would become. And still today I am never really sure of the future, whether the quiet will stretch on for many years or be interrupted by change or cataclysm. There's not much I take for granted.

But the life of a dog is not much of a mystery, really. With few exceptions, he will be who he has always been. His routine will be unvarying and his pleasures will be predictable—a pond, a squirrel, a bone, a nap in the sun. It sounds so boring, and yet it is one of the things that make dogs so important to people. In a world that seems so uncertain, in lives that seem sometimes to ricochet from challenge to upheaval and back again, a dog can be counted on in a way that's true of little else.

There's one other mystery in the lives of people that is not much of a mystery in the life of a dog. That's the question of how long he's going to be with you, although people gloss over this part of the deal most of the time. When we acquired Beau, we got a lot of stuff with him. A red Kong for him to chew, which he never liked as much as chair legs or shoes. A crate for him to sleep in, which he got accustomed to after several nights of tormented keening. A dog Frisbee, which he ignored as it sailed above his head. And a book entitled *Your Labrador Retriever.* The edge of that book is all chewed to bits, and inside is this sentence, "The average life span of a Labrador is twelve years."

Beau died two weeks shy of his fifteenth birth-

day. The five of us knew three days in advance exactly when he would go, which seemed terribly wrong. There are some things that I've never really understood scheduling: a cesarean section, a date night with your husband. But I never felt as bad as I did scheduling the last moments of Beau's life, placing the call to the vet and the crematorium so that both could be ready at nine A.M. on a Monday morning. I never felt as bad as I did turning good old number eleven, for that whole horrible weekend, into a dead dog walking. Or limping, I guess.

I don't know exactly how we settled on that time and day. It's true that we were all together for Christopher's college graduation, that Quin was home from Beijing and Maria from college and that all three of them wanted to be there. The trajectory of Beau's existence had reversed itself: While he once ran off, leaving three children at home to worry and wait, now they had sailed free while he lay by the door, patiently anticipating their return. I knew just how he felt. My husband and I live in a cleaner house now, with only canine company, waiting for the noise, the disruption, and the delight that the return of our three natives brings. The tables have turned for us all.

Maybe it was that his children recognized what we had tried for months not to see: that it was time for Beau to go, too. Over a period of several weeks, what little light was left in the Big Guy's pale, blind eyes had seemed to dim, and when he cried, he no longer seemed to be looking for attention but to be seeking an end to pain. For a long time we had kept him alive because he still had some life in him, some curiosity that made him put his nose to the ground to see what other animal had recently passed his way, some faint scamper to his step when his chow rattled into the bowl, even if the bowl had to be placed right up against his face to show him where to find it.

Then one day we suddenly realized that we had been keeping him alive not because it was good for him, but because it was good for us, because it was too hard to make the decision to let him go. And in

the joyful bargain between dog and person, that is the one unforgivable cheat.

He seemed a little perplexed by all the attention when we gathered around him on the patterned rug, so colorful, so good at hiding doggie stains. I lay next to him on the floor at his head while Dr. Brown, there for that house call, true to her word, positioned herself next to his hind leg. Beau pulled back irritably at the first pinch, then went still again, looking, as ever, dignified and handsome, his head held high. I had my arms around his neck, my face buried in his shoulder, and from above me I felt what I thought for one befuddled moment was rain, the same rain that was falling so hard out on the street, making that stones-in-a-tin-can sound. Then I realized it was my husband's tears. I could hear our children sobbing, and suddenly, improbably, I was almost exultant at the love we had managed to muster for that old dog, and at the thought that someday, if I was very, very lucky, I might have a death as simple and serene as this one, with these same people around me.

People talk nonsense to dogs all the time, the same as they talk to babies. I whispered in his ear over and over again, the way I had when he was a puppy squatting on the grass. "Yes, yes, you are the man," I murmured, "you are the best dog, yes, everything's going to be all right, you are the man." Dr. Brown looked at me and I nodded and she pushed the plunger on the syringe. Beau took two deep growly breaths and then he fell onto me. We had put him down. I don't like euphemisms for death, hate the term "passed away" for someone who has died, but the expression we use for dogs is the right one. We put him down.

I've never really believed what people say, that death smoothes the lines of life away, that the tension and the worry disappear. Yet somehow after the vet had packed up and the children had gone, Beau did look more like his old self, before his legs and eyesight and hearing began to go. He looked more like the kind of dog who would try to drive a horse from his stretch of the road, or swim in circles, his

tail a feathered rudder, in pursuit of geese. He looked like one of those handsome Labs on the cover of a dog book. He looked like what he was: a really good dog.

The life of a good dog is like the life of a good person, only shorter and more compressed. In the fifteen years since Beau had joined our family, nine pounds of belly fat and needle teeth, he had grown ancient by the standards of his breed. And I had grown older. My memory stutters. My knees hurt. Without my reading glasses the words on a page look like ants at a picnic. But my blood pressure is low, my bone scan is good, and my mammograms are so far uneventful. I love my kids, and they love me, and we all love their father, who is still my husband. Starting out, I thought that life was terribly complex, and in some ways it is. But contentment can be pretty simple.

And that's what I learned from watching Beau over his lifetime: to roll with the punches (if not in carrion), to take things as they come, to measure myself not in terms of the past or the future but of the present, to raise my nose in the air from time to time and, at least metaphorically, holler, "I smell bacon!" I'm not what I once was, and neither, by the end, was he. The geese are making a mess of the pond, and the yellow Lab gets to run every morning with her master. The first couple of times she was walked by herself were particularly sad. Bea misses Beau terribly, I suspect, but I may just be projecting again.

Each morning I used to check to see if the old guy was actually breathing, and each day I tried to take his measure—was he hurting? was he happy? Was the trade-off between being infirm and being alive worth it? And when the time comes to ask myself some of those same questions, at least I will have had experience calibrating the answer. Sometimes an old dog teaches you new tricks.

ABOUT THE AUTHOR

ANNA QUINDLEN is the author of five bestselling novels, *Object Lessons, One True Thing, Black and Blue, Blessings,* and *Rise and Shine.* Her *New York Times* column "Public and Private" won a Pulitzer Prize in 1992, and a selection of those columns was published as *Thinking Out Loud.* She is also the author of a collection of her "Life in the 30s" columns, *Living Out Loud;* a book for the Library of Contemporary Thought, *How Reading Changed My Life;* the bestselling *A Short Guide to a Happy Life* and *Being Perfect;* and two children's books, *The Tree That Came to Stay* and *Happily Ever After.* She is currently a columnist for *Newsweek* and lives with her husband, their children, and her Labrador, Bea, in New York City.

The text of this book was set in Filosofia. It was designed in 1996 by Zuzanna Licko, who created it for digital typesetting as an interpretation of the sixteenth-century typeface Bodoni. Filosofia, an example of Licko's unusual font designs, has classical proportions with a strong vertical feeling, softened by rounded droplike serifs. She has designed many typefaces and is the co-founder of *Emigre* magazine, where many of them first appeared. Born in Bratislava, Czechoslovakia, Licko came to the United States in 1968. She studied graphic communications at the University of California at Berkeley, graduating in 1984.